AF530378

I never thought that I would write a book, but here it is. I never thought that my book would have readers, but here you are. Now, we have a special and magical cosmic connection. There are some atoms in this universe which we have set vibrating together. Let's see where they take both of us. For the next few moments, seconds, minutes, hours, years and possibly, a lifetime, a piece of me will now, forever, be a piece of you.

'What stopped you from achieving your dreams?' asked the ant.

'What people might think about me...' answered the little girl.

'What if I die alone?' wondered the little girl.

'You most likely will, but that's not a bad thing,' claimed the ant.

'Which way do I go?' asked the little girl.

'The one that leads you to yourself. Since, that's the path with the most flowers on the way,' told the ant.

'Are we lost?' quizzed the little girl.

'Yes we are. We are lost in the beauty of this world,' replied the ant.

'What amazes you the most about your relationships?' asked the ant.

'How everyone leaves a piece of themselves inside me after they leave... I wonder if I leave a little bit of myself in others too.' quipped the little girl.

'You do,' replied the ant.

'Who is your competition?'
said the little girl.

'My own self... Today, I want to be better than what I was yesterday,' answered the lioness.

'And your inspiration?'
probed the little girl.

'All the great things I'm capable of being.'
Said the lioness

'What are you most afraid of?' asked the little girl.

'My mind... It plays so many tricks on me,' responded the lioness.

'What do you love the most about the journey?' asked the elephant.

'All the strangers I meet on the way. They have become my friends and I will remember them forever,' answered the little girl.

'Aww, That is so sweet. My dear, are you in love with someone?' questioned the elephant.

'Absolutely! I am deeply and truly in love with myself,' quipped the little girl.

'Oh look, there's a cheese platter there!' exclaimed the elephant.

The ant watched with eyes wide open!

'Life is always better with lots of cheese and a garnish of friendship,' said the wise lioness.

'Interesting! But, what would you do if there was only one slice of cheese and two of us? Would you split it in half?' asked the elephant.

'I wouldn't need to, silly! I trust that nose of yours to find more for us,' laughed the little girl.

'Elephant... You're the largest land animal, you really have nothing to fear,' said the little girl.

'I fear the little ants...' whispered the elephant.

'Trust me,' urged the ant.

'How? You can kill me if you want to!' exclaimed the elephant.

'I can also save your life. I know the way back home,' said the ant.

'I will try to trust you. Together, we're a force to reckon with,' claimed the elephant.

'Oh look, I can fly,' said the lioness.
'How did you not know that before?'
wondered the little girl.

'Sometimes, I forget the most
important thing: To believe in myself,'
responded the lioness.

'Tell me, where are we headed?' asked the lioness.

'Home.' Answered the little girl.

'And where's that?' asked the lioness.
'Um... I'm still figuring that out,' replied the girl.

'For me, it's where all the cheese and crackers are,' chimed in the elephant.

'I feel most at home when we are all together,' said the ant.

'I am my own home,' announced the lioness.

'Oh look, is that home?' asked the little girl.

'No silly, that's cheese and crackers. But it's like a home for your mouth,' laughed the ant.

'Look! There's a light there. Is that home?' asked the little girl.

'Oh darling! You don't need to look for that. There's a bright light inside you too,' said the lioness.

'I found something that's better than cheese and crackers,' said the ant.

'Is it cheese and wine?' asked the elephant.

'Yes! That and good company makes things so much easier,' said the ant.

'They don't call you the queen of jungle out of fear. To be a queen, you need to earn their love,' said the lioness.

'Trophallaxis, I have two stomachs. One for myself and one for sharing with my friends and family,' claimed the ant.

'An elephant always remembers... And that's not always a good thing,' sighed the elephant.

'What even? Are you a lioness or something else?' said the elephant.

'Well, I'm a lot of things. But you can only see what you choose to see.,' said the lioness.

'Life is always tough, but you see,
there will always be different
types of cheese to try,'
spoke the elephant.

'Look! I can store so much water in my trunk!' trumeted the elephant.

'Wow! See, I can carry fifty times my weight!' hummed the ant.

'I can fly,' howled the lioness.

'I don't really know what I can do,' said the girl.

'You're here with us. Nothing will ever be the same without you. That's your superpower,' answered the ant.

'Some people wouldn't ever imagine all of us together. Love and kindness helped us to be friends with each other,' said the ant.

'What's the most extraordinary thing in this world?' wondered the girl.

'Love and kindness. They work like magic!' enlightened the ant.